EASY GUITAR
WITH NOTES & TAB

BEST OF Chuck Berry

T007173&

Cover photo © Michael Ochs Archives/Getty Images

ISBN 978-1-4803-8440-8

HAL•LEONARD®
CORPORATION
7777 W. BLUEMOUND RD. P.O. BOX 13819 MILWAUKEE, WI 53213

In Australia Contact:
Hal Leonard Australia Pty. Ltd.
4 Lentara Court
Cheltenham, Victoria, 3192 Australia
Email: ausadmin@halleonard.com.au

Visit Hal Leonard Online at
www.halleonard.com

STRUM AND PICK PATTERNS

This chart contains the suggested strum and pick patterns that are referred to by number at the beginning of each song in this book. The symbols ⊓ and ∨ in the strum patterns refer to down and up strokes, respectively. The letters in the pick patterns indicate which right-hand fingers play which strings.

p = thumb
i = index finger
m = middle finger
a = ring finger

For example; Pick Pattern 2
is played: thumb - index - middle - ring

Strum Patterns   ## Pick Patterns

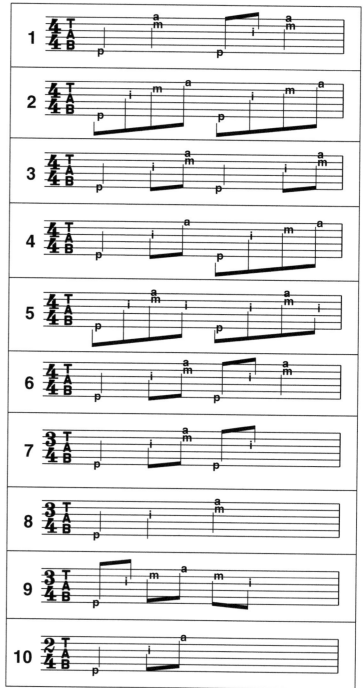

You can use the 3/4 Strum and Pick Patterns in songs written in compound meter (6/8, 9/8, 12/8, etc.). For example, you can accompany a song in 6/8 by playing the 3/4 pattern twice in each measure. The 4/4 Strum and Pick Patterns can be used for songs written in cut time (¢) by doubling the note time values in the patterns. Each pattern would therefore last two measures in cut time.

BEST OF Chuck Berry

Back in the U.S.A.

Words and Music by Chuck Berry

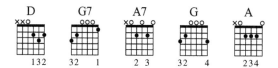

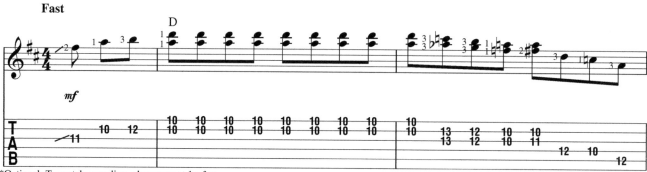

*Capo I

Strum Pattern: 6
Pick Pattern: 1

Intro
Fast

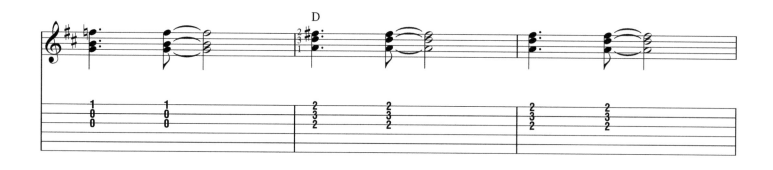

*Optional: To match recording, place capo at 1st fret.

%Verse

1. Oh well, _____ oh well, ___ I feel so good ___ to - day. _
3. *Piano Solo*
5. *See additional lyrics*

We just touched ground on an

in - ter - nat - 'nal run - way, _____ jet - pro -

pelled back home ___ from o - ver - seas to the U. S. A. _____

Verse

2. New York, _____ Los An - ge - les, oh, how I yearned for you. _
4., 6. *See additional lyrics*

De - troit,   Chi - ca - go,

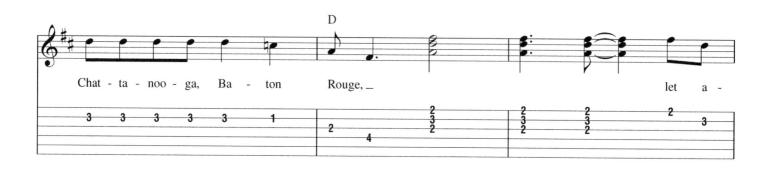

Chat - ta - noo - ga,   Ba - ton   Rouge, __   let a-

3rd time, To Coda ⊕

lone   just   to   be   at   my   home   back   in   old   Saint   Lou. __

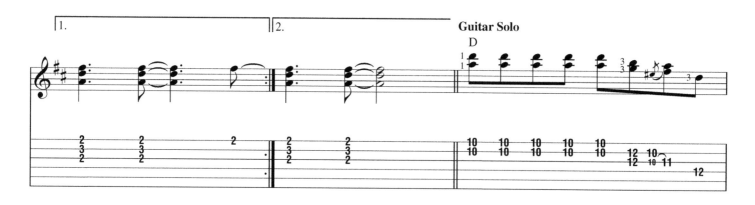

1.   2.   **Guitar Solo**

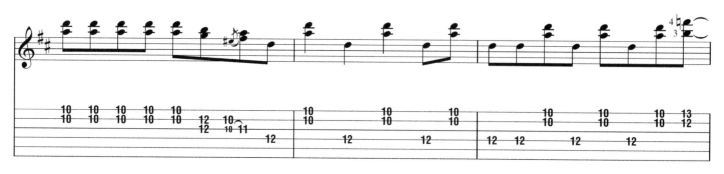

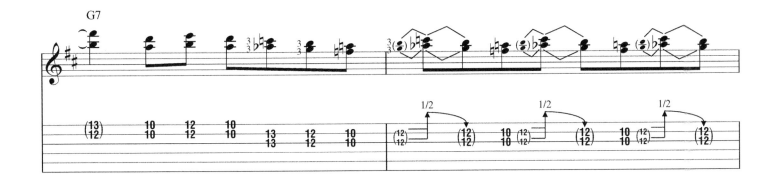

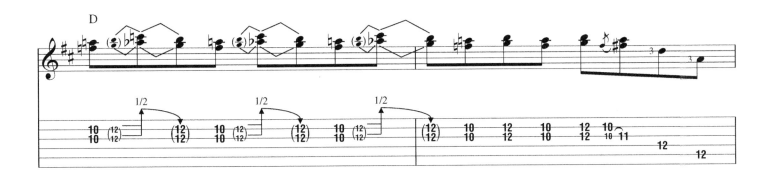

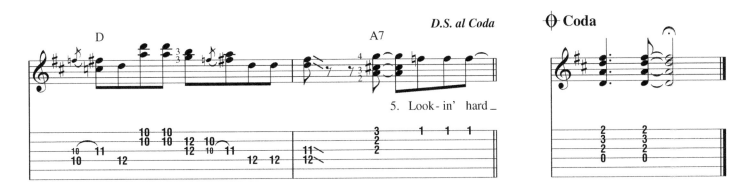

Additional Lyrics

4. Did I miss the skyscrapers, did I miss the long freeway?
   From the coast of California to the shores of the Delaware Bay,
   You can bet your life I did till I got back in the U.S.A.

5. Lookin' hard for a drive-in, searchin' for a corner café
   Where hamburgers sizzle on an open grill, night and day,
   Yeah, and a jukebox jumpin' with records like in the U.S.A.

6. Well, I'm so glad I'm livin' in the U.S.A.
   Yes, I'm so glad I'm livin' in the U.S.A.
   Anything you want, they got it right here in the U.S.A.

Carol
(O Carole)
Words and Music by Chuck Berry

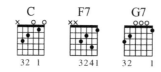

Strum Pattern: 5
Pick Pattern: 1

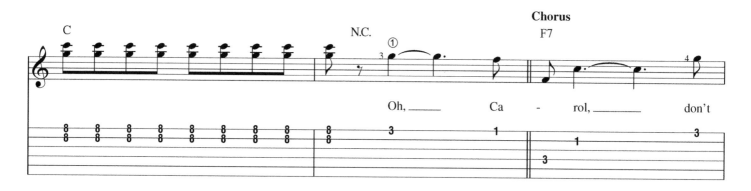

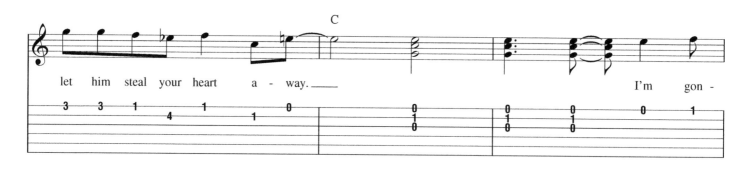

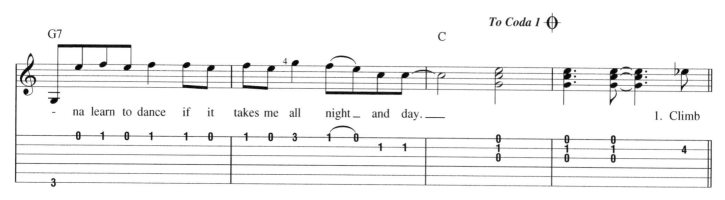

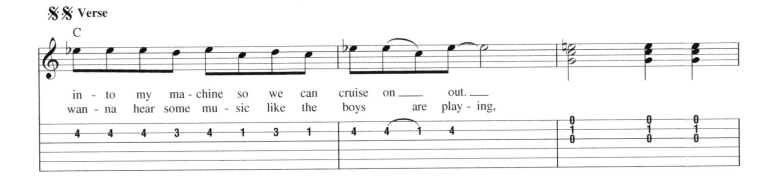

in - to my ma - chine so we can cruise on _____ out. _____
wan - na hear some mu - sic like the boys are play - ing,

I know a swing - in' lit - tle joint where we can jump and shout. _____
hold tight, ___ pat your foot, don't let 'em car - ry it a - way. _____

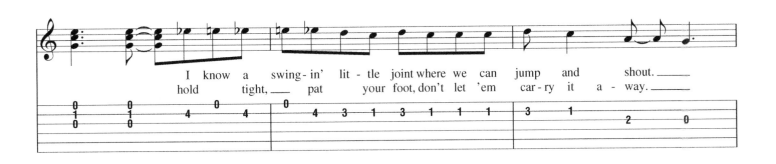

It's not too far back off the high - way, not so
Don't let the heat o - ver - come you when they

long a ride. ___
play so loud. ___ You park your
Well, don't the

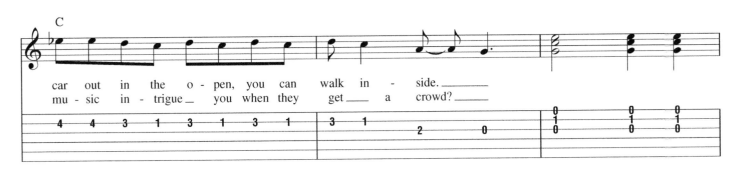

car out in the o - pen, you can walk in - side. _____
mu - sic in - trigue_ you when they get ___ a crowd? _____

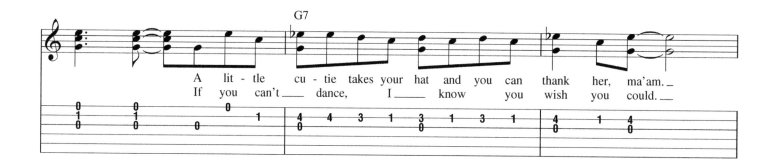

A lit - tle cu - tie takes your hat and you can thank her, ma'am. ___
If you can't ___ dance, I ___ know can you wish you could. ___

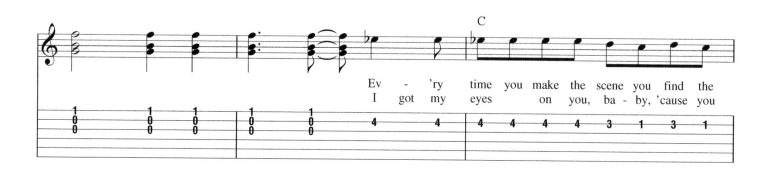

Ev - 'ry time you make the scene you find the
I got my eyes on you, ba - by, 'cause you

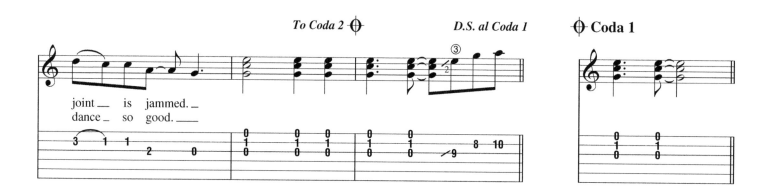

To Coda 2 ⊕   *D.S. al Coda 1*   ⊕ **Coda 1**

joint ___ is jammed. ___
dance ___ so good. ___

Interlude

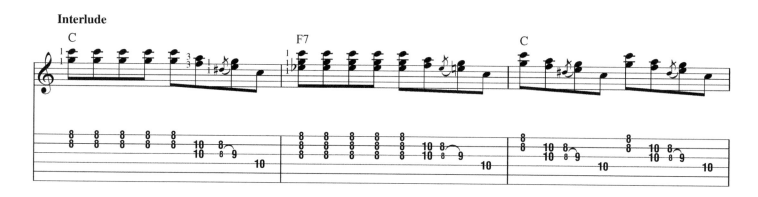

Guitar Solo

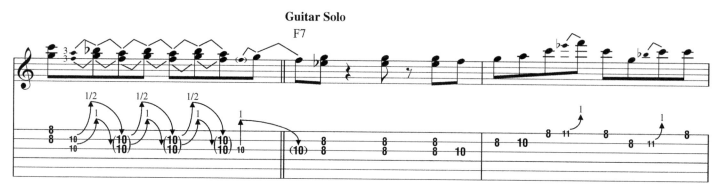

Johnny B. Goode

Words and Music by Chuck Berry

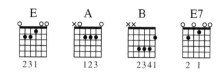

*Capo VI

Strum Pattern: 1
Pick Pattern: 4

Intro

Fast

*Optional: To match recording, place capo at 6th fret.

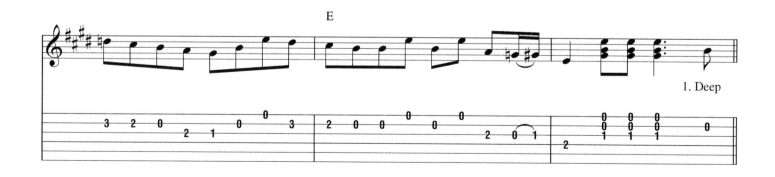

1. Deep

down   in   Lou - 'si - an - a,   close   to   New   Or - leans, ___   way

2., 3. *See additional lyrics*

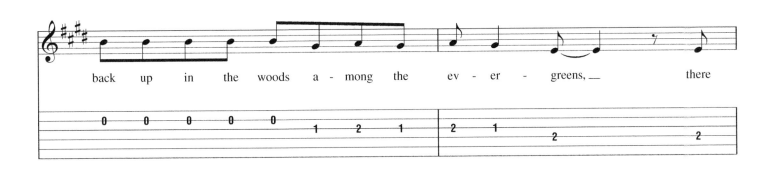

back   up   in   the   woods   a - mong   the   ev - er - greens, ___   there

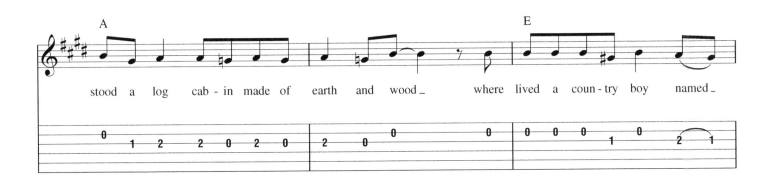

stood   a   log   cab - in   made   of   earth   and   wood ___   where   lived   a   coun - try   boy   named ___

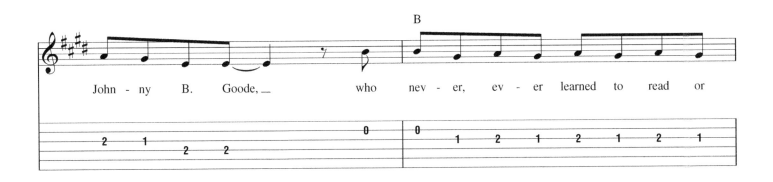

John - ny   B.   Goode, ___   who   nev - er,   ev - er   learned   to   read   or

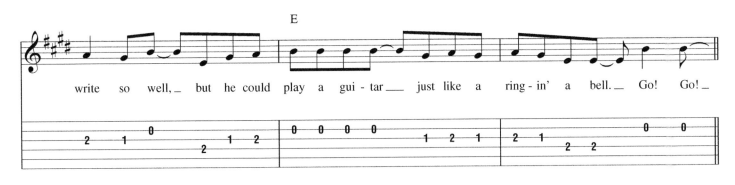

write   so   well, ___   but   he   could   play   a   gui - tar ___   just   like   a   ring - in'   a   bell. ___   Go!   Go! ___

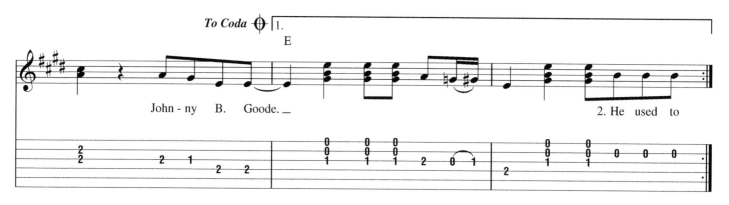

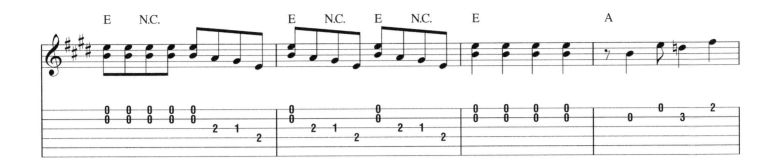

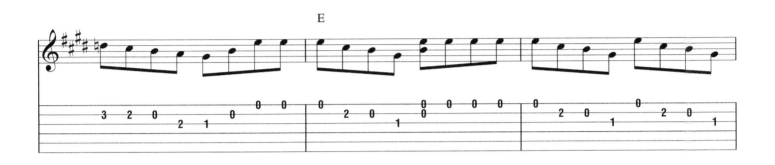

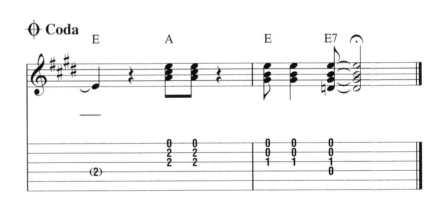

Additional Lyrics

2. He used to carry his guitar in a gunny sack,
   Go sit beneath the tree by the railroad track.
   Old engineers would see him sittin' in the shade,
   Strummin' with the rhythm that the drivers made.
   When people passed by him they would stop and say,
   "Oh my, but that little country boy could play."

3. His mother told him, "Someday you will be a man,
   And you will be the leader of a big ol' band.
   Many people comin' from miles around
   Will hear you play your music when the sun go down.
   Maybe some day your name will be in lights,
   Sayin', "Johnny B. Goode tonight."

Maybellene

Words and Music by Chuck Berry

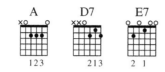

*Capo I

Strum Pattern: 1
Pick Pattern: 5

Intro
  Moderately, in 2

*Optional: To match recording, place capo at 1st fret.

Chorus

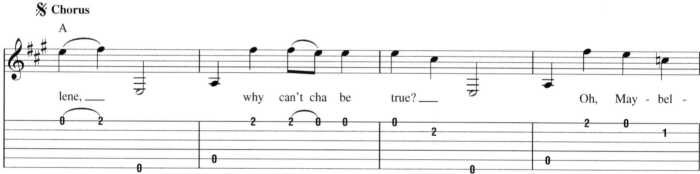

lene, ___ why can't cha be true? ___ Oh, May - bel -

lene, why can't cha be true? You done

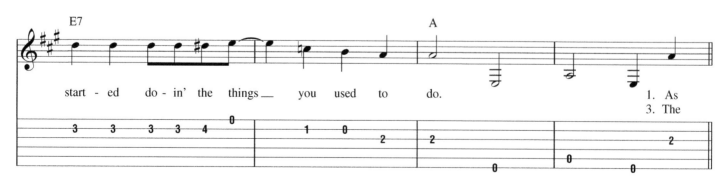

start - ed do - in' the things ___ you used to do.

1. As
3. The

Verse

I was mo-ti-vat-in' o-ver the hill, __ I saw May-bel-lene in a
Cad-il-lac pulled up to 'hun-dred and four, __ the Ford got hot and would-n't
mo-tor cooled down, the heat went down, and that's when I heard that high-

Coupe de Ville; __ a Cad-il-lac a roll-in' on a o-pen road.
do no mo'. __ It done got cloud-y and start-ed to rain. __ I
-way sound. __ The Cad-il-lac set-tin' like a ton o' lead, __ a

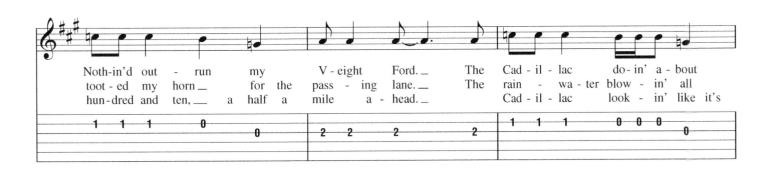

Noth-in'd out-run my V-eight Ford. __ The Cad-il-lac do-in' a-bout
toot-ed my horn __ for the pass-ing lane. __ The rain-wa-ter blow-in' all
hun-dred and ten, __ a half a mile a-head. __ Cad-il-lac look-in' like it's

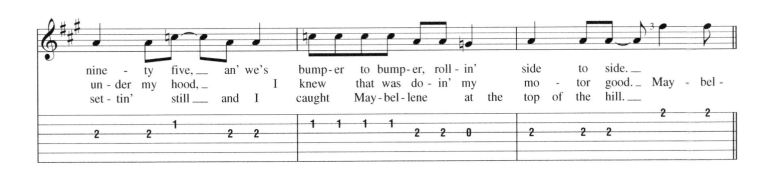

nine-ty five, __ an' we's bump-er to bump-er, roll-in' side to side. __ May-bel-
un-der my hood, __ I knew that was do-in' my mo-tor good. __ May-bel-
set-tin' still __ and I caught May-bel-lene at the top of the hill. __

Chorus

lene, why can't cha be true? __ Oh, May-bel-

lene,   why can't cha be true?   You done

3rd time, To Coda

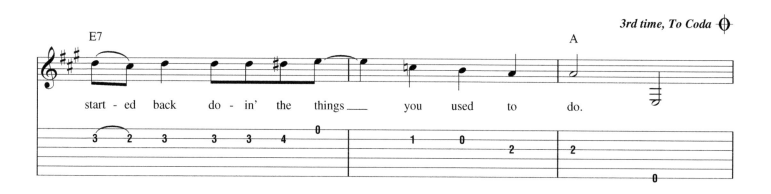

start - ed back do - in' the things ____ you used to do.

Guitar Solo

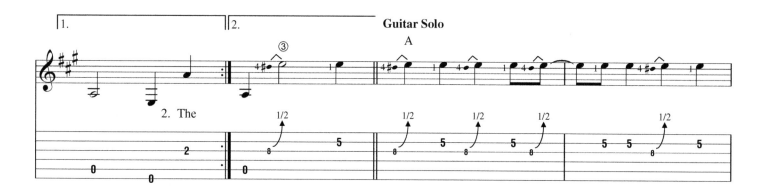

2. The

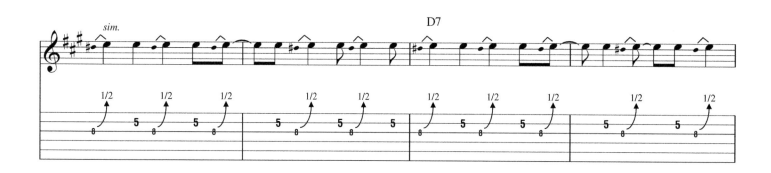

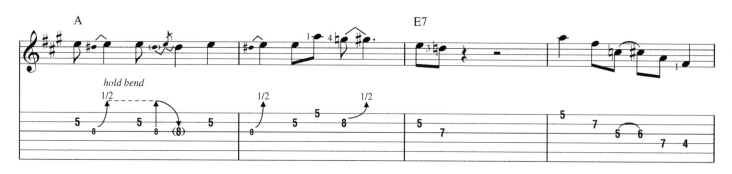

hold bend

Memphis, Tennessee

Words and Music by Chuck Berry

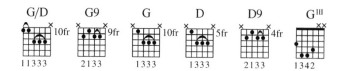

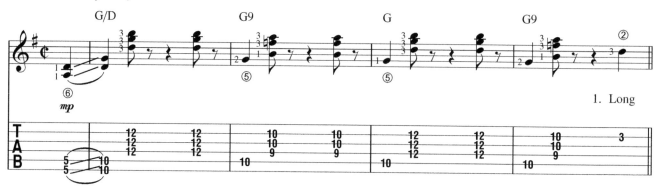

Strum Pattern: 1
Pick Pattern: 5

Intro
Moderately slow, in 2

1. Long

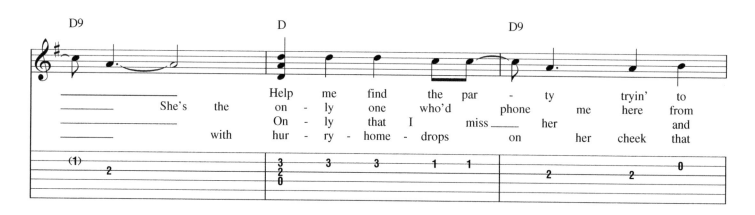

2. Help me, in - for - ma - tion, get in touch with my Ma - rie.
3. Help me, in - for - ma - tion, more than that I can - not add.
4. Last time I saw Ma - rie, she's wav - ing me good - bye

dis - tance in - for - ma - tion, give me Mem - phis, Ten - nes - see.

She's the
Help me find the par - ty tryin' to
On - ly one who'd phone me here from
Only that I miss her and
with hur - ry - home - drops on her cheek that

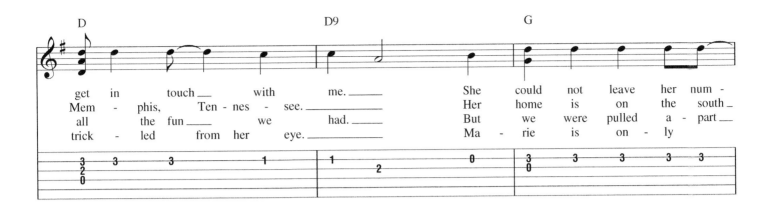

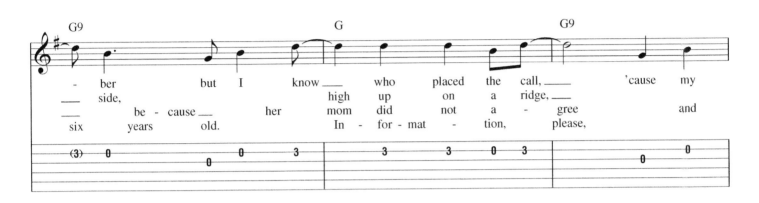

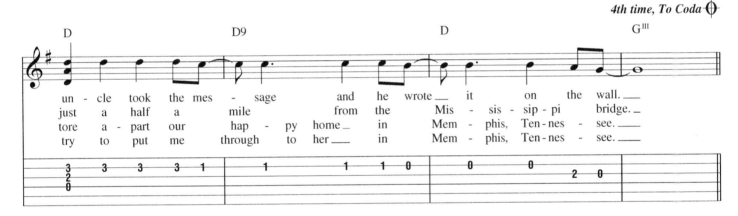

Interlude

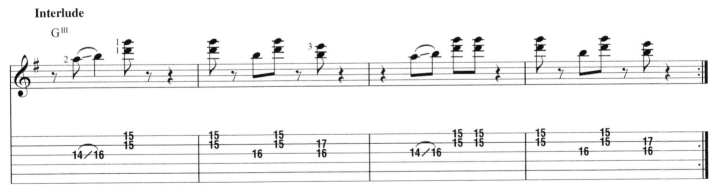

Guitar Solo

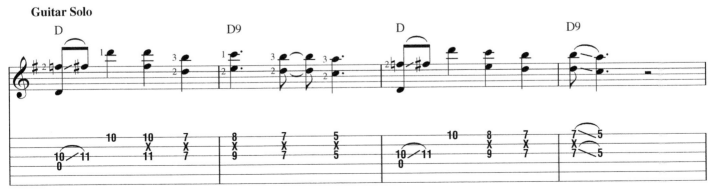

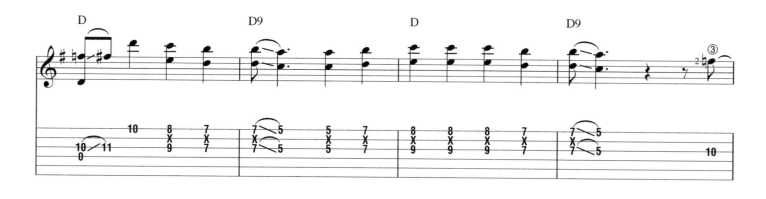

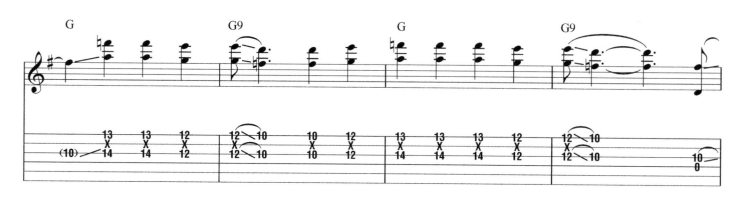

Interlude

D.S. al Coda
(take repeat)

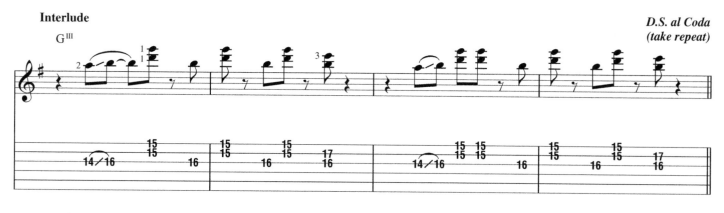

⟡ Coda

Outro

Repeat and fade

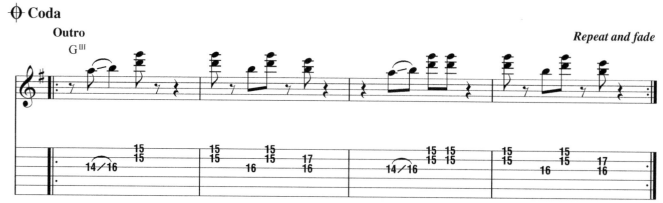

Nadine (Is It You)

Words and Music by Chuck Berry

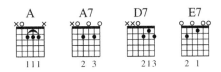

*Capo I

Strum Pattern: 3
Pick Pattern: 3

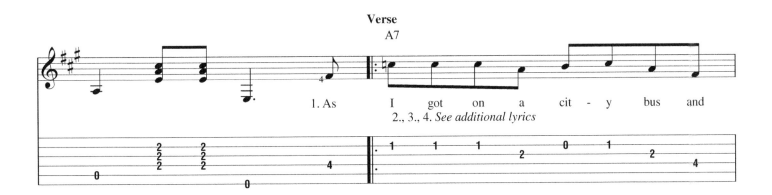

*Optional: To match recording, place capo at 1st fret.

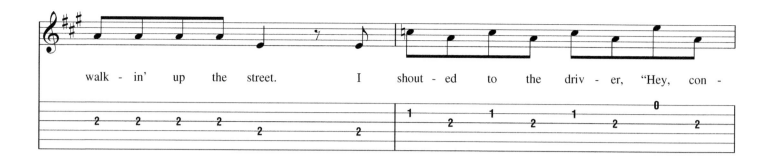

walk - in' up the street. I shout - ed to the driv - er, "Hey, con -

duc - tor, you must slow down, I think I see her, please let me off the bus." Na - dine,

𝄋 **Chorus**

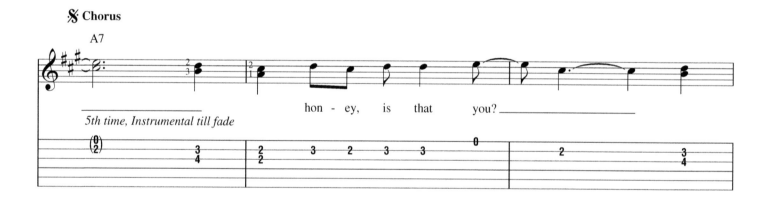

5th time, Instrumental till fade

hon - ey, is that you?

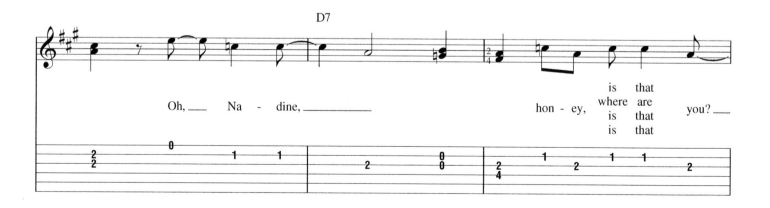

Oh, Na - dine,

hon - ey, where are you?
is that
is that

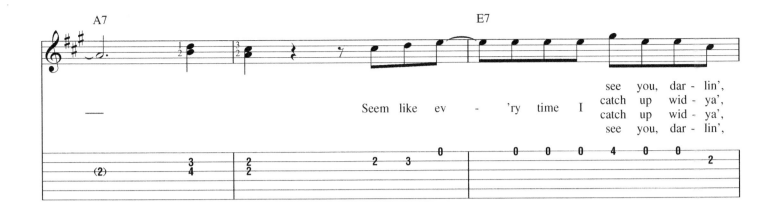

Seem like ev - 'ry time I   see you, dar - lin',
                      catch up wid - ya',
                      catch up wid - ya',
                      see you, dar - lin',

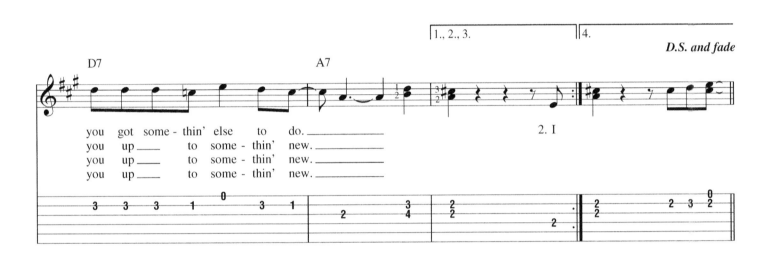

1., 2., 3.   **4.**

D.S. and fade

you got some - thin' else to do. ___
you up ___ to some - thin' new. ___
you up ___ to some - thin' new. ___
you up ___ to some - thin' new. ___

2. I

Additional Lyrics

2. I saw her from the corner when she turned and doubled back,
   She started walkin' toward a coffee-colored Cadillac.
   I's pushin' through the crowd, try'n' to get to where she was at
   And I was campaign shoutin' like a southern diplomat.

3. Downtown searching for her, looking all around.
   Saw her getting in a yellow cab, heading uptown.
   I caught a loaded taxi, paid up everybody's tab.
   Flipped a twenty dollar bill and told them, "Catch that yellow cab."

4. She moves around like a wayward summer breeze.
   Go, driver, go. Go catch her for me please.
   Moving through the traffic like a mounted cavalier.
   Leaning out the taxi window tryin' to make her hear.

My Ding-a-Ling

Words and Music by Dave Bartholomew and Sam Rhodes

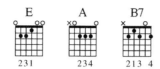

*Tune down 1/2 step:
(low to high) E♭-A♭-D♭-G♭-B♭-E♭

Strum Pattern: 3
Pick Pattern: 3

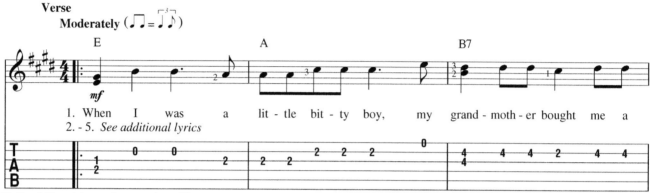

*Optional: To match recording, tune down 1/2 step.

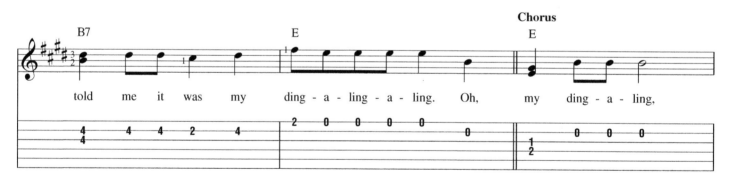

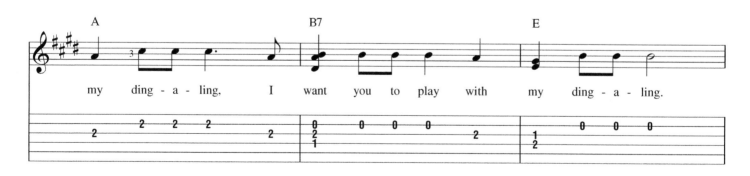

My ding - a - ling, my ding - a - ling, I want you to play with

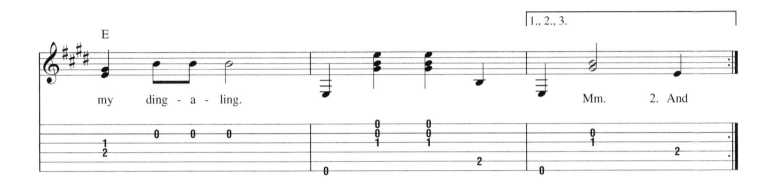

my ding - a - ling. Mm. 2. And

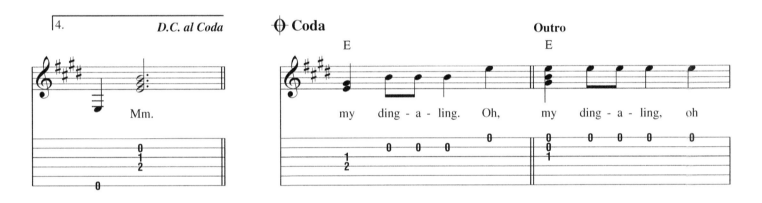

4. ***D.C. al Coda*** ⊕ **Coda** **Outro**

Mm. my ding - a - ling. Oh, my ding - a - ling, oh

Slower

my ding - a - ling, I want to play with my ding - a - ling!

Additional Lyrics

2. And then Mama took me to grammar school,
   But I stopped off in the vestibule.
   Ev'ry time that bell would ring,
   Catch me playin' with my ding-a-ling-a-ling.

3. Once I was climbing the garden wall,
   I slipped and had a terrible fall.
   I fell so hard, I heard bells ring,
   But held on to my ding-a-ling-a-ling.

4. Once I was swimmin' 'cross Turtle Creek,
   Man, them snappers all around my feet.
   Sho' was hard swimmin' 'cross that thing
   With both hands holdin' my ding-a-ling-a-ling.

5. This here song, it ain't so sad,
   The cutest little song you ever had.
   Those of you who will not sing,
   You must be playin' with your own ding-a-ling.

Reelin' and Rockin'

Words and Music by Chuck Berry

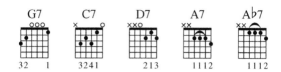

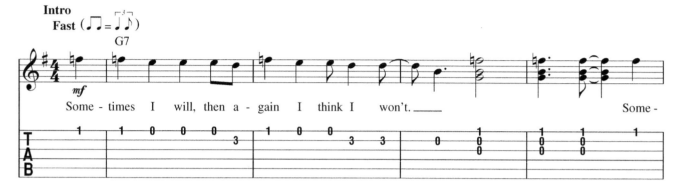

Strum Pattern: 5
Pick Pattern: 1

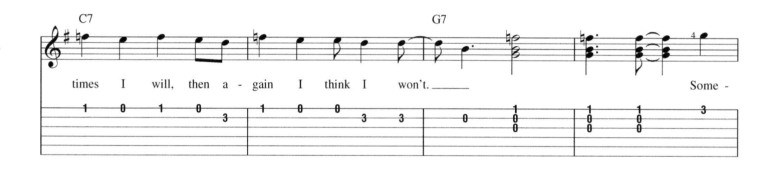

Some - times I will, then a - gain I think I won't.____ Some -

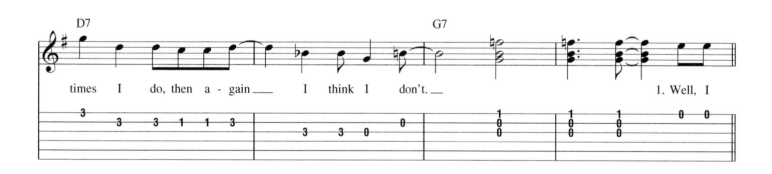

times I will, then a - gain I think I won't._____ Some -

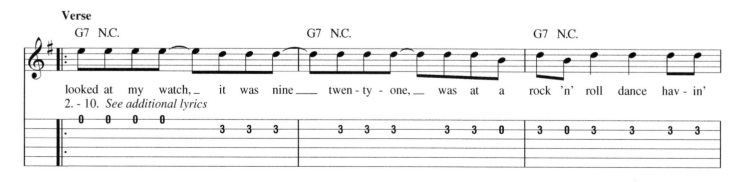

times I do, then a - gain ____ I think I don't. ___ 1. Well, I

looked at my watch, ___ it was nine ____ twen - ty - one, ___ was at a rock 'n' roll dance hav - in'
2. - 10. *See additional lyrics*

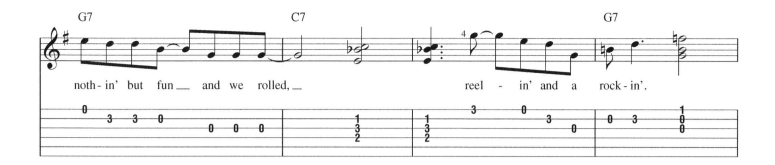

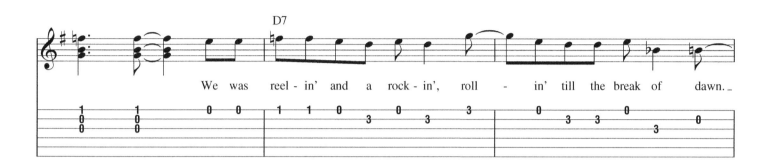

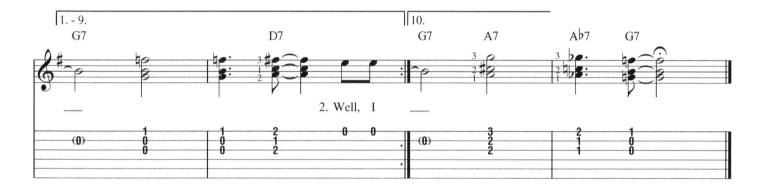

Additional Lyrics

2. Well, I looked at my watch, it was nine thirty-two,
   There's nothin' I'd rather do than dance with you,
   And we rolled, reelin' and a rockin'.
   We was reelin' and a rockin' way till the break of dawn.

3. Well, I looked at my watch, it was nine forty-three,
   And ev'ry time I'd spin, she'd spin with me,
   And we reeled, reelin' and a rockin'.
   We was reelin' and a rockin', rollin' till the break of dawn.

4. Well, I looked at my watch, it was nine fifty-four.
   I said, "Dance, ballerina girl, go go go!"
   And we rolled, reelin' and a rockin'.
   We was reelin' and a rockin', rollin' till the break of dawn.

5. Well, I looked at my watch, it was ten o five,
   Man, I didn't know wheth'r I was dead or alive
   And I's rollin', reelin' and a rockin'.
   We was reelin' and a rockin', rollin' till the break of dawn.

6. Well, I looked at my watch, it was ten twenty-six,
   But I'm a keep on dancin' till I get my kicks,
   And we reeled, reelin' and a rockin'.
   We was reelin' and a rockin', rollin' till the break of dawn.

7. Well, I looked at my watch, it was ten twenty-eight.
   I gotta get my kicks 'fore it get too late,
   And we reeled, reelin' and a rockin'.
   We was reelin' and a rockin', rollin' till the break of dawn.

8. Well, I looked at my watch, it was ten twenty-nine,
   I had to hold her hand, she is still holdin' mine,
   And we reeled, reelin' and a rockin'.
   We was reelin' and a rockin', rollin' till the break of dawn.

9. Well, I looked at my watch, and, to my surprise,
   I was dancing with a woman that was twice my size.
   I was reelin', reelin' and a rockin'.
   I was reelin' and a rockin', rollin' till the break of dawn.

10. Well I looked at my watch and it was time to go.
    The bandleader said, "We ain't playin' no mo,"
    And we was reelin', reelin' and a rockin'.
    We was reelin' and a rockin' way till the break of dawn.

Rock and Roll Music

Words and Music by Chuck Berry

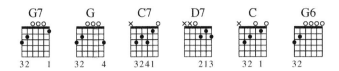

*Capo VIII

Strum Pattern: 3
Pick Pattern: 3

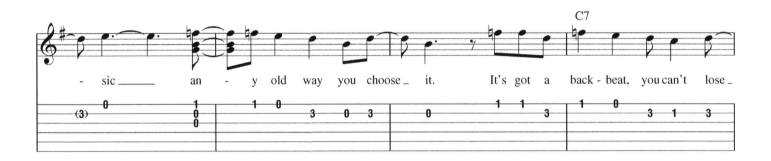

*Optional: To match recording, place capo at 8th fret.

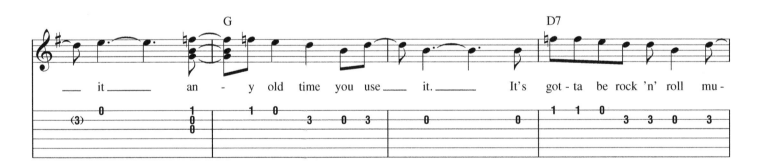

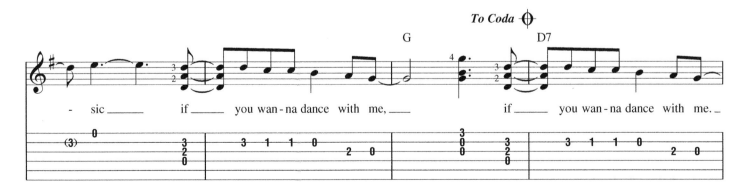

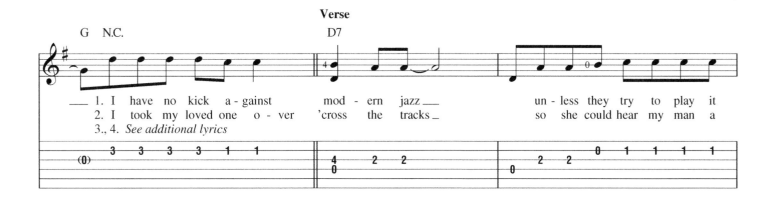

Verse

1. I have no kick a-gainst modern jazz ___ un-less they try to play it
2. I took my loved one o-ver 'cross the tracks ___ so she could hear my man a
3., 4. *See additional lyrics*

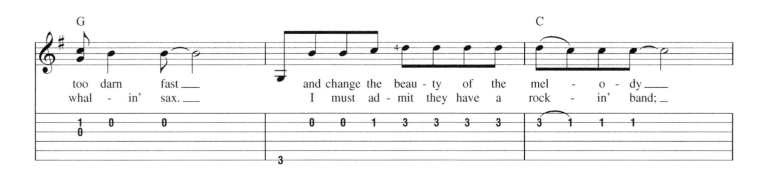

too darn fast ___ and change the beau-ty of the mel - o - dy ___
whal - in' sax. ___ I must ad - mit they have a rock - in' band; ___

4th time, D.S. al Coda

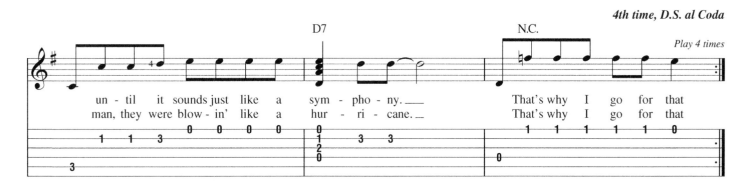

Play 4 times

un - til it sounds just like a sym - pho - ny. ___ That's why I go for that
man, they were blow - in' like a hur - ri - cane. ___ That's why I go for that

Coda

___ you wan - na dance with me. ___

Additional Lyrics

3. Way down south they gave a jubilee,
   Them country folks, they had a jamboree.
   They're drinkin' home brew from a wooden cup,
   The folks dancin' got all shook up
   And started playin' that...

4. Don't care to hear 'em play a tango.
   I'm in no mood to dig a mambo.
   It's way too early for the congo,
   So keep a rockin' that piano
   So I can hear some of that...

Roll Over Beethoven

Words and Music by Chuck Berry

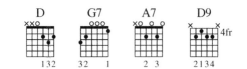

*Capo I

Strum Pattern: 5
Pick Pattern: 1

Intro
Very fast

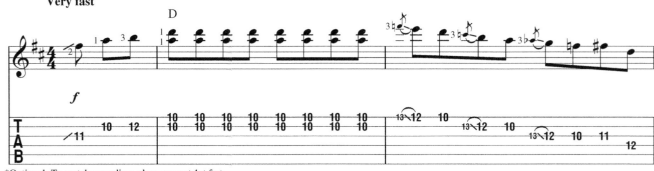

*Optional: To match recording, place capo at 1st fret.

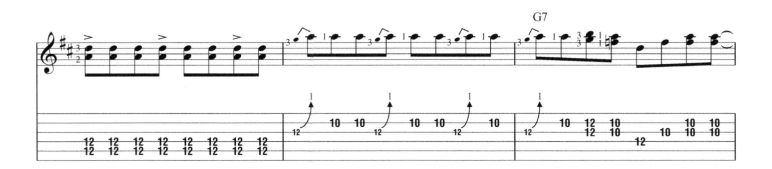

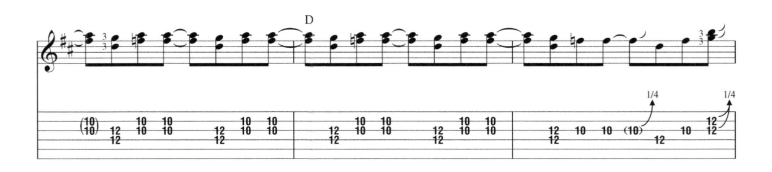

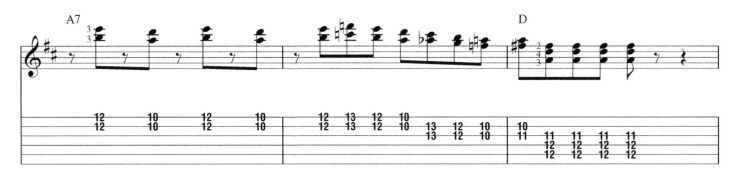

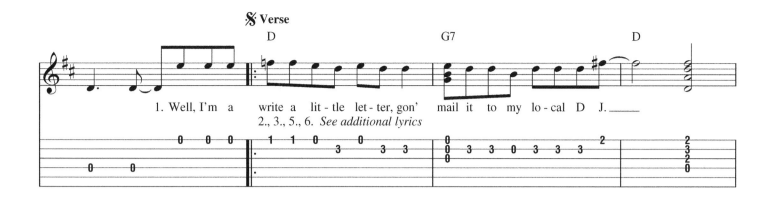

5th time, To Coda

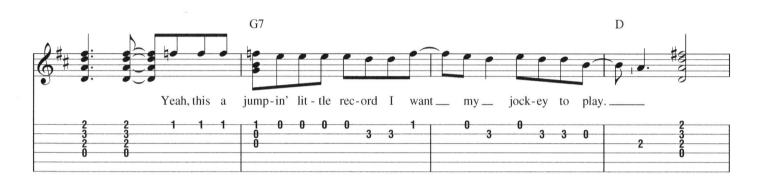

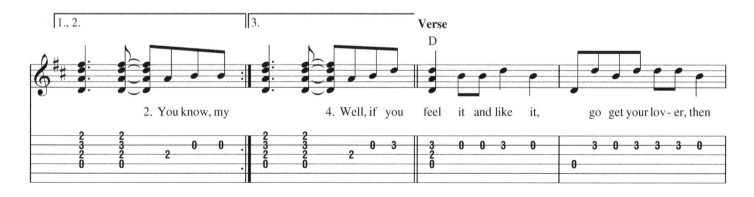

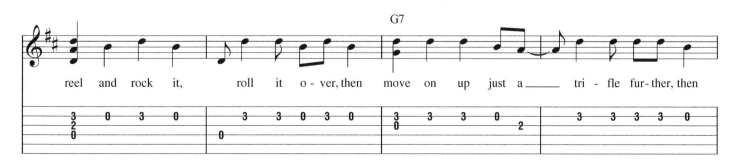

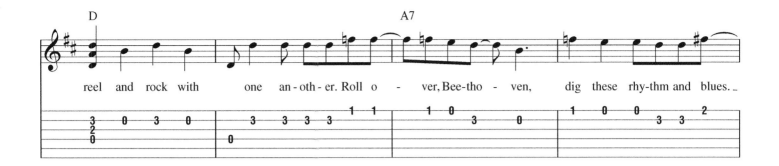

reel and rock with one an-oth-er. Roll o - ver, Bee-tho - ven, dig these rhy-thm and blues.

Guitar Solo

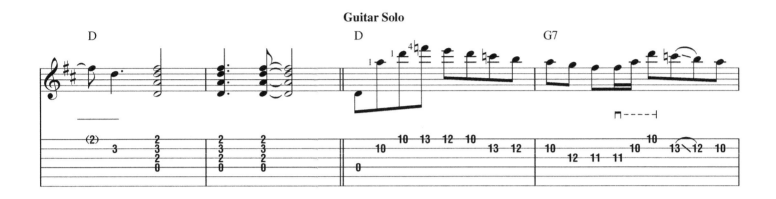

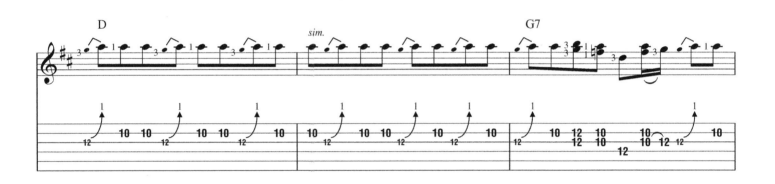

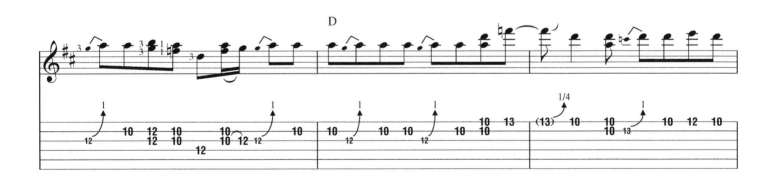

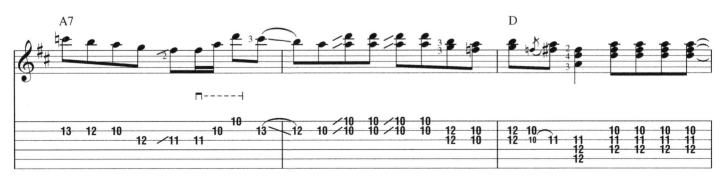

Additional Lyrics

2. You know, my temp'rature risin', the jukebox blowin' a fuse.
   My heart beatin' rhythm and my soul keep a singin' the blues.
   A, roll over, Beethoven, tell Tchaikovsky the news.

3. I got the rockin' pneumonia; I need a shot of rhythm and blues.
   I caught the rollin' arthritis sittin' down at a rhythm review.
   A, roll over, Beethoven, they're rockin' in two by two.

5. Well, early in the mornin' and I'm givin' you my warnin',
   Don't you step on my blue suede shoes.
   Hey, diddle diddle, I'm a playin' my fiddle,
   Ain't got nothin' to lose.
   Roll over, Beethoven, tell Tchaikovsky the news.

6. You know, she wiggle like a glowworm, dance like a spinning top.
   She got a crazy partner, you ought to see 'em reel and rock.
   Long as she got a dime, the music won't never stop.

School Day
(Ring! Ring! Goes the Bell)

Words and Music by Chuck Berry

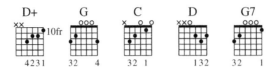

D+   G   C   D   G7

Strum Pattern: 1
Pick Pattern: 1

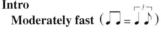

Intro
Moderately fast

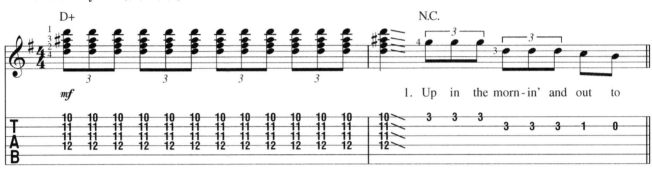

1. Up in the morn-in' and out to

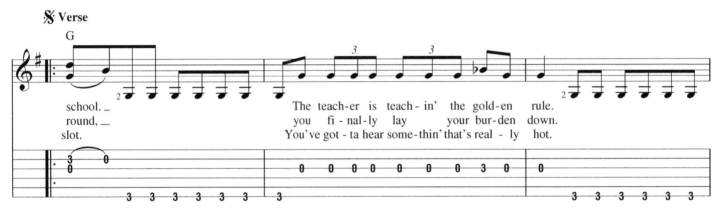

school. _ The teach-er is teach-in' the gold-en rule.
round, _ you fi-nal-ly lay your bur-den down.
slot. You've got-ta hear some-thin' that's real-ly hot.

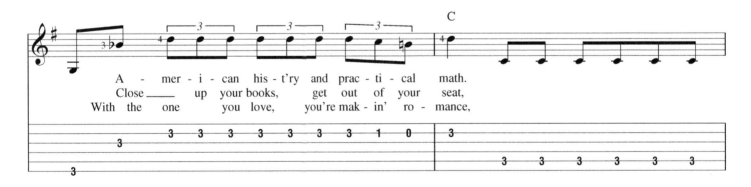

A-mer-i-can his-t'ry and prac-ti-cal math.
Close _ up your books, get out of your seat,
With the one you love, you're mak-in' ro-mance,

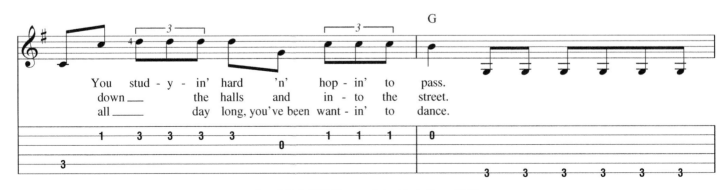

You stud-y-in' hard 'n' hop-in' to pass.
down _ the halls and in-to the street.
all _ day long, you've been want-in' to dance.

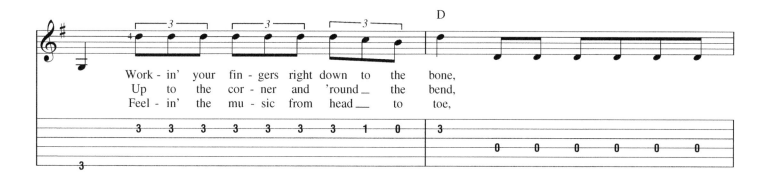

Work - in' your fin - gers right down to the bone,
Up to the cor - ner and 'round __ the bend,
Feel - in' the mu - sic from head __ to toe,

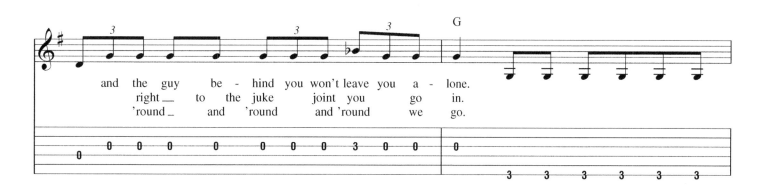

and the guy be - hind you won't leave you a - lone.
right __ to the juke joint you go in.
'round __ and 'round and 'round we go.

Verse

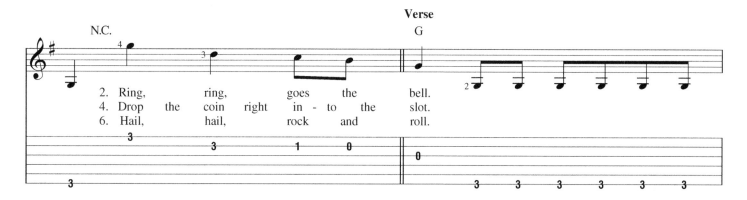

2. Ring, ring, goes the bell.
4. Drop the coin right in - to the slot.
6. Hail, hail, rock and roll.

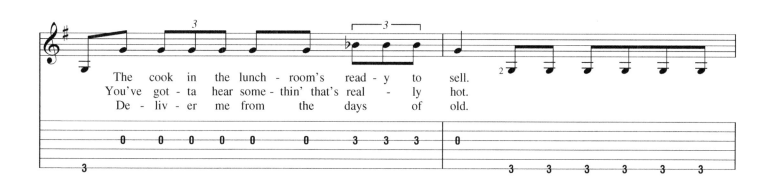

The cook in the lunch - room's read - y to sell.
You've got - ta hear some - thin' that's real - ly hot.
De - liv - er me from the days of old.

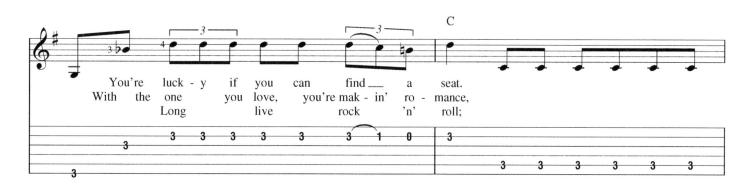

You're luck - y if you can find __ a seat.
With the one you love, you're mak - in' ro - mance,
Long live rock 'n' roll;

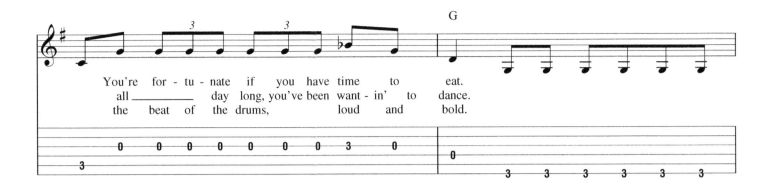

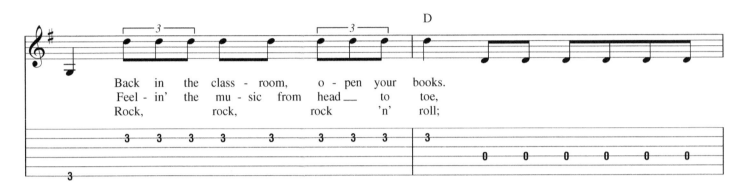

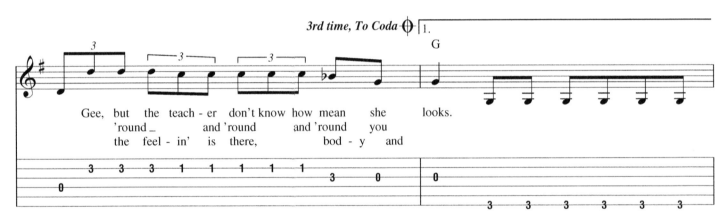

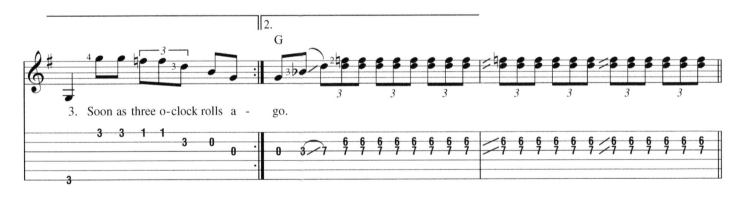

Guitar Solo

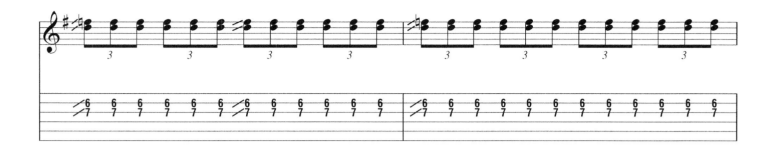

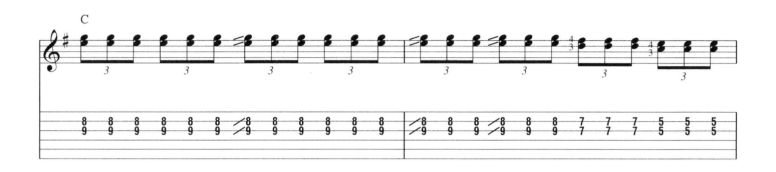

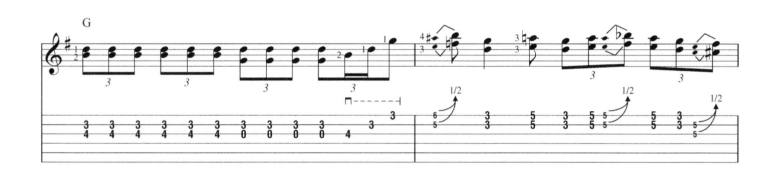

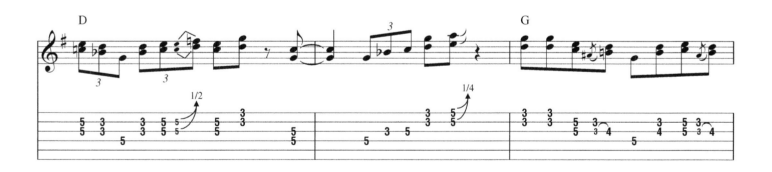

D.S. al Coda   Coda

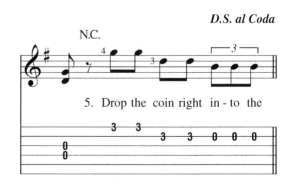

5. Drop the coin right in - to the

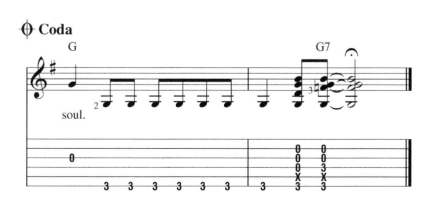

soul.

Sweet Little Rock and Roller

Words and Music by Chuck Berry

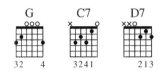

Strum Pattern: 3
Pick Pattern: 3

Intro
Moderately fast

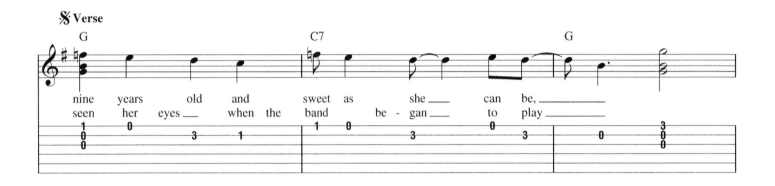

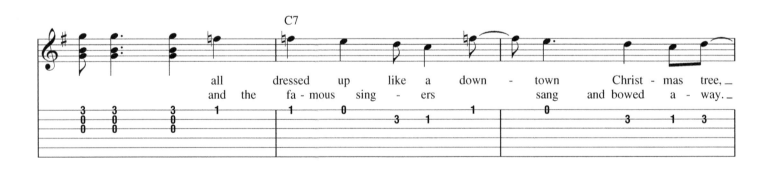

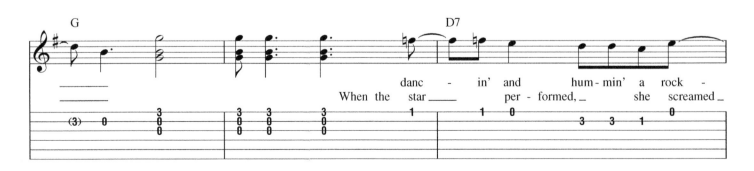

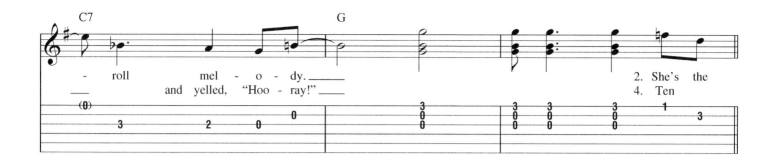

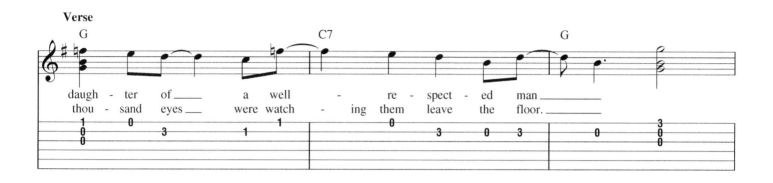

Verse

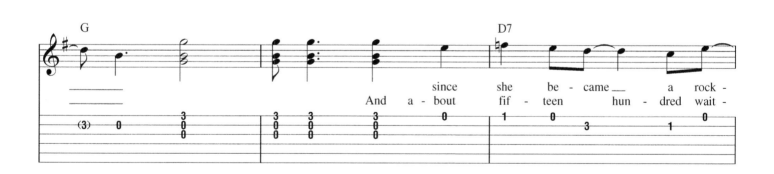

To Coda ⊕

Chorus

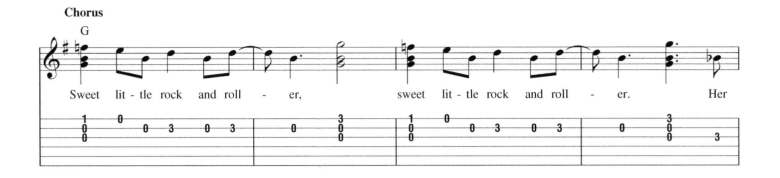

Sweet lit - tle rock and roll — er, sweet lit - tle rock and roll — er. Her

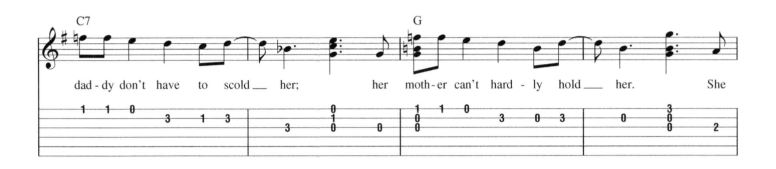

dad - dy don't have to scold — her; her moth - er can't hard - ly hold — her. She

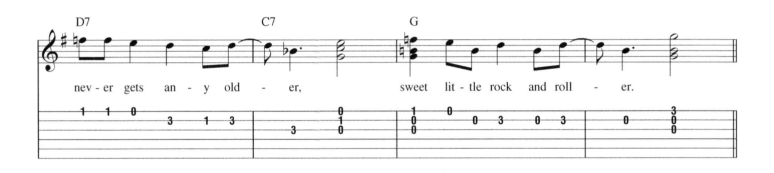

nev - er gets an - y old — er, sweet lit - tle rock and roll — er.

Guitar Solo

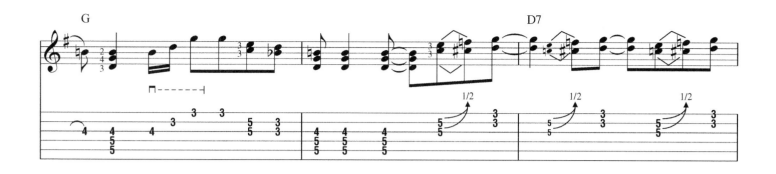

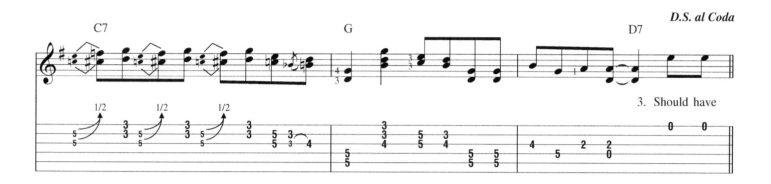

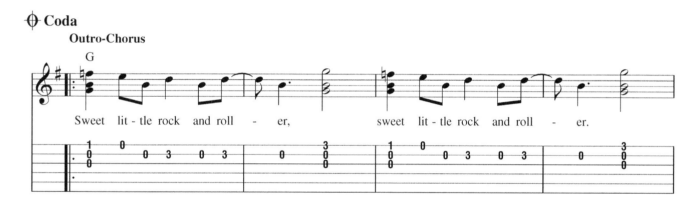

3. Should have

⊕ Coda

Outro-Chorus

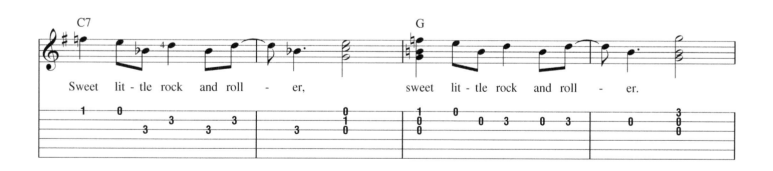

Sweet lit - tle rock and roll - er, sweet lit - tle rock and roll - er.

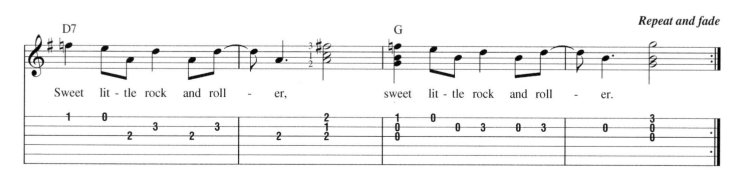

Sweet lit - tle rock and roll - er, sweet lit - tle rock and roll - er.

Repeat and fade

Sweet lit - tle rock and roll - er, sweet lit - tle rock and roll - er.

Sweet Little Sixteen

Words and Music by Chuck Berry

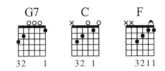

*Capo I

Strum Pattern: 1
Pick Pattern: 1

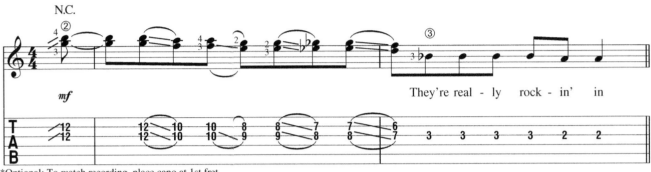

*Optional: To match recording, place capo at 1st fret.

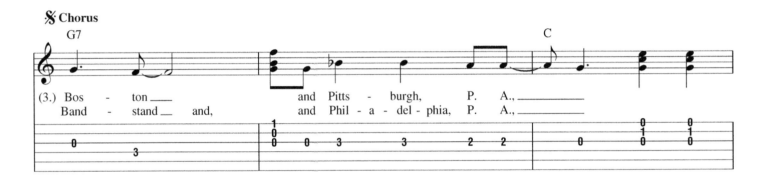

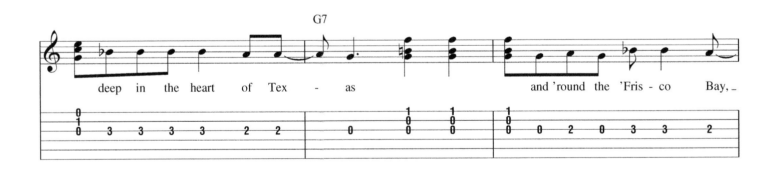

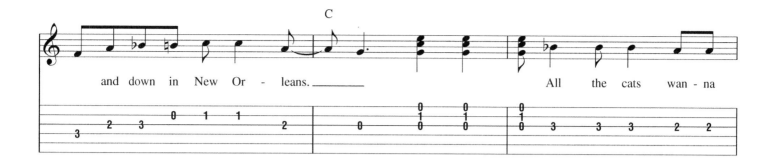

and down in New Or - leans. _____ All the cats wan-na

3rd time, To Coda 2

dance with ___ sweet lit - tle six - teen. _____

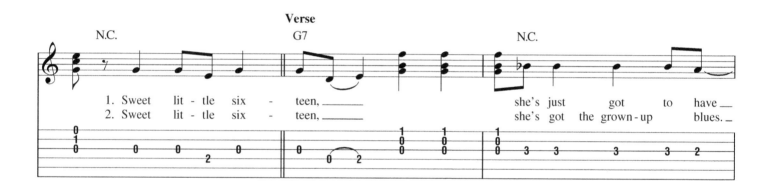

Verse

1. Sweet lit - tle six - teen, _____ she's just got to have ___
2. Sweet lit - tle six - teen, _____ she's got the grown - up blues. _

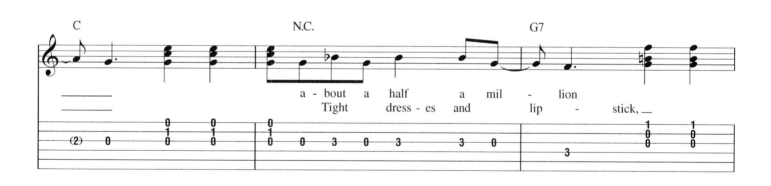

_____ a - bout a half a mil - lion
_____ Tight dress - es and lip - stick, __

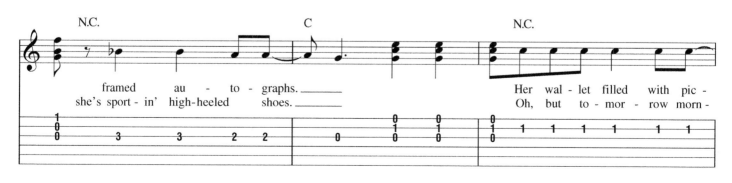

framed au - to - graphs. _____ Her wal - let filled with pic -
she's sport - in' high - heeled shoes. _____ Oh, but to - mor - row morn -

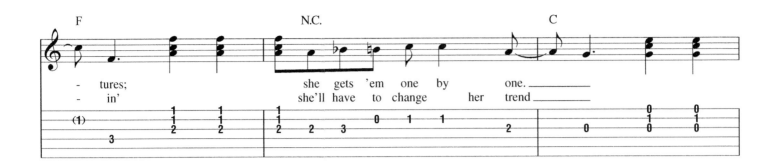

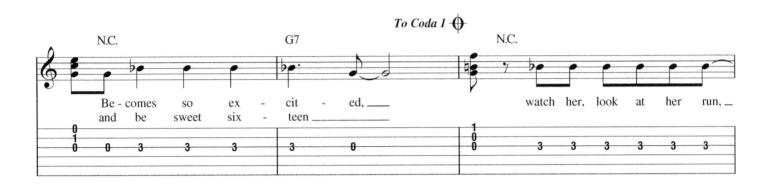

Oh, Dad - dy, Dad - dy, _____ I beg ____ of you, _____

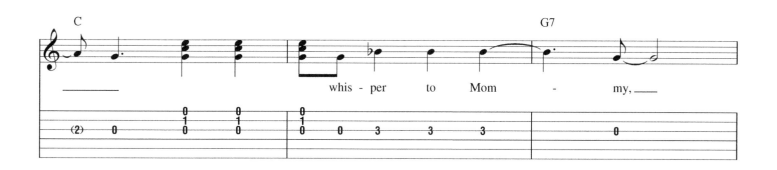

_____ whis - per to Mom - my, _____

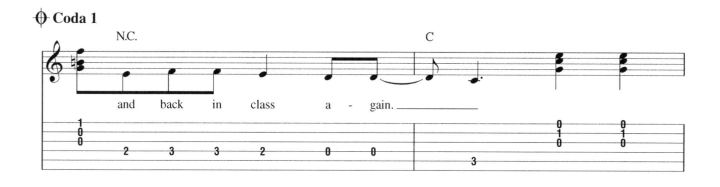

D.S. al Coda 1

it's al - right with you. _____ 'Cause they'll be rock - in' on

Coda 1

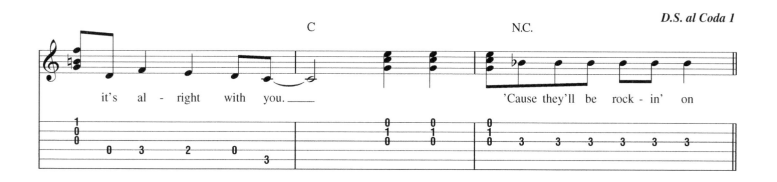

and back in class a - gain. _____

D.S. al Coda 2 **Coda 2**

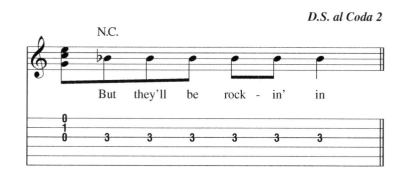

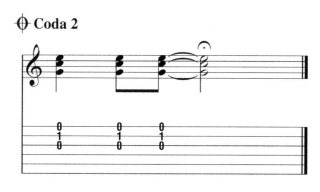

But they'll be rock - in' in

You Never Can Tell

Words and Music by Chuck Berry

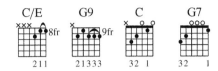

Strum Pattern: 3
Pick Pattern: 3

Intro
Fast

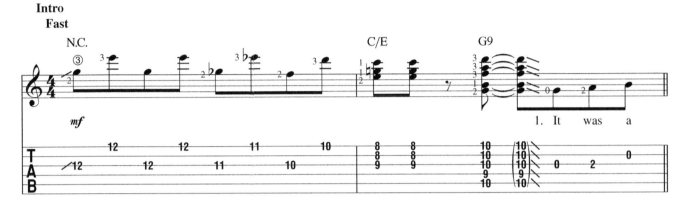

1. It was a

Verse

(6.) teen - age wed - ding and the old folks wished 'em well. _____
2., 3., 4. *See additional lyrics*
5., 7. *Instrumental*

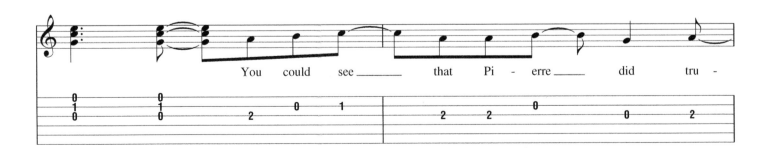

You could see _____ that Pi - erre _____ did tru -

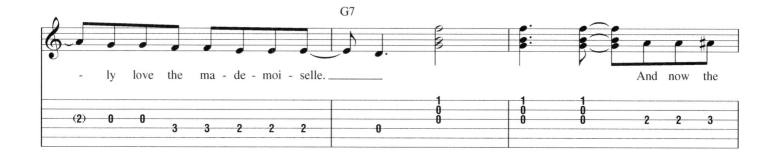

-ly love the ma-de-moi-selle._____ And now the

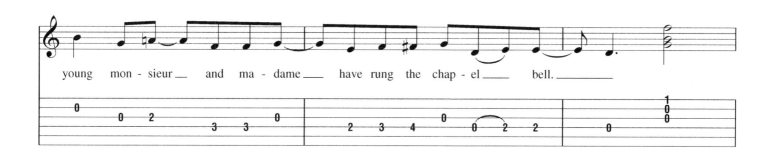

young mon-sieur__ and ma-dame__ have rung the chap-el ___ bell._____

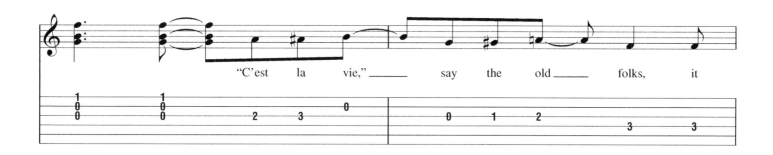

"C'est la vie,"_____ say the old ___ folks, it

Play 7 times and fade

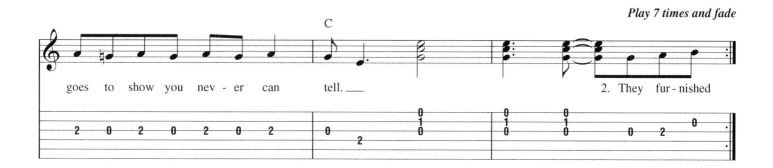

goes to show you nev-er can tell.___ 2. They fur-nished

Additional Lyrics

2. They furnished off an apartment with a two room Roebuck sale.
   The coolerator was crammed with TV dinners and ginger ale.
   But when Pierre found work, the little money comin' worked out well.
   "C'est la vie," say the old folks, it goes to show you never can tell.

3. They had a hi-fi phono, boy, did they let it blast.
   Seven hundred little records, all rock, rhythm and jazz.
   But when the sun went down, the rapid tempo of the music fell.
   "C'est la vie," say the old folks, it goes to show you never can tell.

4. They bought a souped-up jitney, was a cherry red fifty-three,
   And drove it down to Orleans to celebrate their anniversary.
   It was there where Pierre was wedded to the lovely mademoiselle.
   "C'est la vie," say the old folks, it goes to show you never can tell.

No Particular Place to Go

Words and Music by Chuck Berry

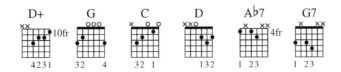

Strum Pattern: 1
Pick Pattern: 1

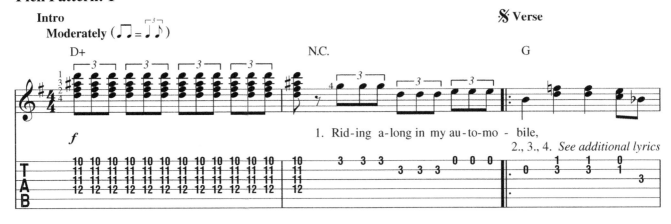

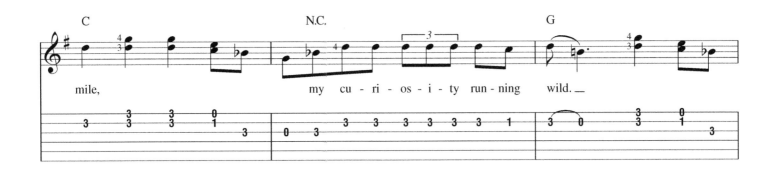

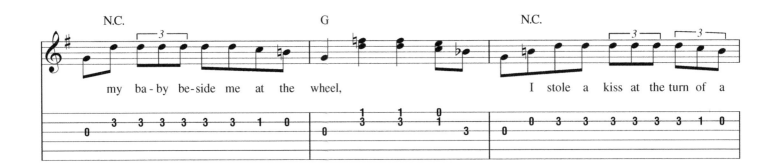

go.   2. Rid-ing a-long in my au-to-mo -   go.

Guitar Solo

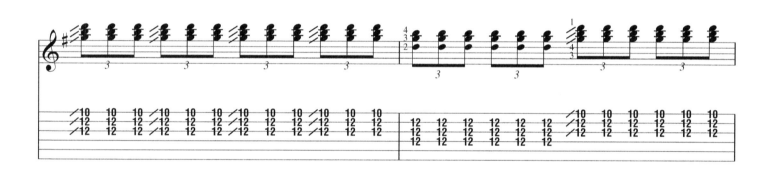

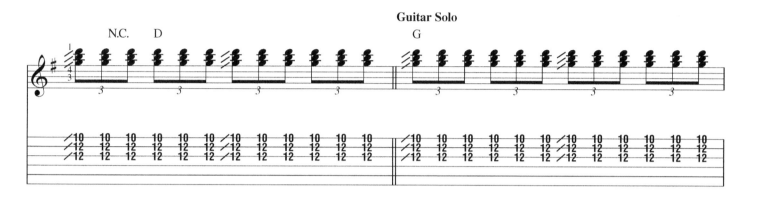

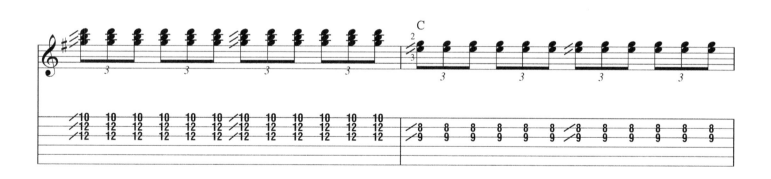

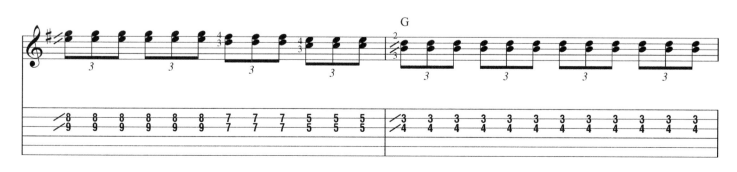

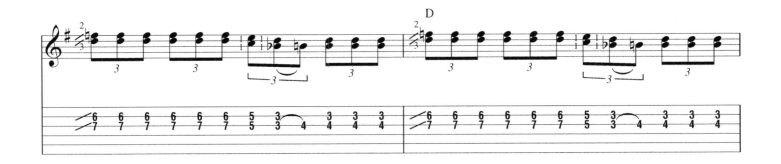

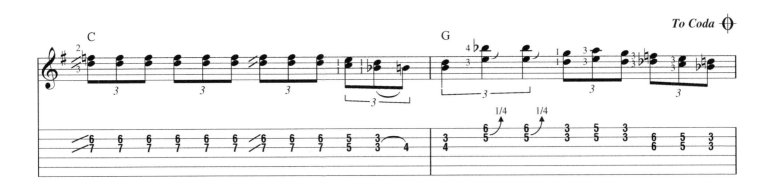

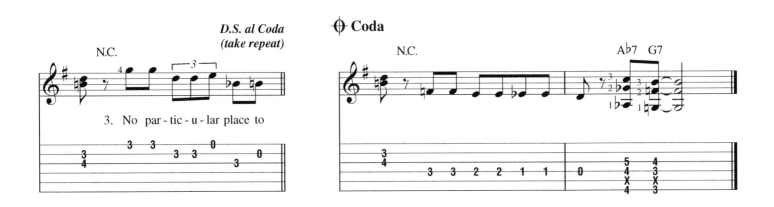

Additional Lyrics

2. Riding along in my automobile,
   I was anxious to tell her the way I feel.
   So I told her softly and sincere
   And she leaned and whispered in my ear.
   Cuddling more and driving slow,
   With no particular place to go.

3. No particular place to go,
   So we parked way out on the cocamo.
   The night was young and the moon was gold,
   So we both decided to take a stroll.
   Can you imagine the way I felt?
   I couldn't unfasten her safety belt.

4. Riding along in my calaboose,
   Still trying to get her belt a loose.
   All the way home, I held a grudge
   For the safety belt that wouldn't budge.
   Cruising and playing the radio
   With no particular place to go.

This series features simplified arrangements with notes, tab, chord charts, and strum and pick patterns.

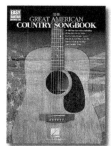  

MIXED FOLIOS

00702287	Acoustic	$19.99
00702002	Acoustic Rock Hits for Easy Guitar	$15.99
00702166	All-Time Best Guitar Collection	$19.99
00702232	Best Acoustic Songs for Easy Guitar	$16.99
00119835	Best Children's Songs	$16.99
00703055	The Big Book of Nursery Rhymes & Children's Songs	$16.99
00698978	Big Christmas Collection	$19.99
00702394	Bluegrass Songs for Easy Guitar	$15.99
00289632	Bohemian Rhapsody	$19.99
00703387	Celtic Classics	$14.99
00224808	Chart Hits of 2016-2017	$14.99
00267383	Chart Hits of 2017-2018	$14.99
00334293	Chart Hits of 2019-2020	$16.99
00702149	Children's Christian Songbook	$9.99
00702028	Christmas Classics	$8.99
00101779	Christmas Guitar	$14.99
00702141	Classic Rock	$8.95
00159642	Classical Melodies	$12.99
00253933	Disney/Pixar's Coco	$16.99
00702203	CMT's 100 Greatest Country Songs	$34.99
00702283	The Contemporary Christian Collection	$16.99
00196954	Contemporary Disney	$19.99
00702239	Country Classics for Easy Guitar	$24.99

00702257	Easy Acoustic Guitar Songs	$16.99
00702041	Favorite Hymns for Easy Guitar	$12.99
00222701	Folk Pop Songs	$17.99
00126894	Frozen	$14.99
00333922	Frozen 2	$14.99
00702286	Glee	$16.99
00702160	The Great American Country Songbook	$19.99
00702148	Great American Gospel for Guitar	$14.99
00702050	Great Classical Themes for Easy Guitar	$9.99
00275088	The Greatest Showman	$17.99
00148030	Halloween Guitar Songs	$14.99
00702273	Irish Songs	$12.99
00192503	Jazz Classics for Easy Guitar	$16.99
00702275	Jazz Favorites for Easy Guitar	$17.99
00702274	Jazz Standards for Easy Guitar	$19.99
00702162	Jumbo Easy Guitar Songbook	$24.99
00232285	La La Land	$16.99
00702258	Legends of Rock	$14.99
00702189	MTV's 100 Greatest Pop Songs	$34.99
00702272	1950s Rock	$16.99
00702271	1960s Rock	$16.99
00702270	1970s Rock	$19.99
00702269	1980s Rock	$15.99
00702268	1990s Rock	$19.99
00369043	Rock Songs for Kids	$14.99

00109725	Once	$14.99
00702187	Selections from O Brother Where Art Thou?	$19.99
00702178	100 Songs for Kids	$14.99
00702515	Pirates of the Caribbean	$17.99
00702125	Praise and Worship for Guitar	$14.99
00287930	Songs from *A Star Is Born, The Greatest Showman, La La Land*, and More Movie Musicals	$16.99
00702285	Southern Rock Hits	$12.99
00156420	Star Wars Music	$16.99
00121535	30 Easy Celtic Guitar Solos	$16.99
00702156	3-Chord Rock	$12.99
00244654	Top Hits of 2017	$14.99
00283786	Top Hits of 2018	$14.99
00702294	Top Worship Hits	$17.99
00702255	VH1's 100 Greatest Hard Rock Songs	$34.99
00702175	VH1's 100 Greatest Songs of Rock and Roll	$29.99
00702253	Wicked	$12.99

ARTIST COLLECTIONS

00702267	AC/DC for Easy Guitar	$16.99
00702598	Adele for Easy Guitar	$15.99
00156221	Adele – 25	$16.99
00702040	Best of the Allman Brothers	$16.99
00702865	J.S. Bach for Easy Guitar	$15.99
00702169	Best of The Beach Boys	$15.99
00702292	The Beatles – 1	$22.99
00125796	Best of Chuck Berry	$15.99
00702201	The Essential Black Sabbath	$15.99
00702250	blink-182 — Greatest Hits	$17.99
02501615	Zac Brown Band — The Foundation	$17.99
02501621	Zac Brown Band — You Get What You Give	$16.99
00702043	Best of Johnny Cash	$17.99
00702090	Eric Clapton's Best	$16.99
00702086	Eric Clapton — from the Album Unplugged	$17.99
00702202	The Essential Eric Clapton	$17.99
00702053	Best of Patsy Cline	$15.99
00222697	Very Best of Coldplay – 2nd Edition	$16.99
00702229	The Very Best of Creedence Clearwater Revival	$16.99
00702145	Best of Jim Croce	$16.99
00702278	Crosby, Stills & Nash	$12.99
14042809	Bob Dylan	$15.99
00702276	Fleetwood Mac — Easy Guitar Collection	$17.99
00139462	The Very Best of Grateful Dead	$16.99
00702136	Best of Merle Haggard	$16.99
00702227	Jimi Hendrix — Smash Hits	$19.99
00702288	Best of Hillsong United	$12.99
00702236	Best of Antonio Carlos Jobim	$15.99
00702245	Elton John — Greatest Hits 1970–2002	$19.99

00129855	Jack Johnson	$16.99
00702204	Robert Johnson	$14.99
00702234	Selections from Toby Keith — 35 Biggest Hits	$12.95
00702003	Kiss	$16.99
00702216	Lynyrd Skynyrd	$16.99
00702182	The Essential Bob Marley	$16.99
00146081	Maroon 5	$14.99
00121925	Bruno Mars – Unorthodox Jukebox	$12.99
00702248	Paul McCartney — All the Best	$14.99
00125484	The Best of MercyMe	$12.99
00702209	Steve Miller Band — Young Hearts (Greatest Hits)	$12.95
00124167	Jason Mraz	$15.99
00702096	Best of Nirvana	$16.99
00702211	The Offspring — Greatest Hits	$17.99
00138026	One Direction	$17.99
00702030	Best of Roy Orbison	$17.99
00702144	Best of Ozzy Osbourne	$14.99
00702279	Tom Petty	$17.99
00102911	Pink Floyd	$17.99
00702139	Elvis Country Favorites	$19.99
00702293	The Very Best of Prince	$19.99
00699415	Best of Queen for Guitar	$16.99
00109279	Best of R.E.M.	$14.99
00702208	Red Hot Chili Peppers — Greatest Hits	$16.99
00198960	The Rolling Stones	$17.99
00174793	The Very Best of Santana	$16.99
00702196	Best of Bob Seger	$16.99
00146046	Ed Sheeran	$15.99
00702252	Frank Sinatra — Nothing But the Best	$12.99
00702010	Best of Rod Stewart	$17.99
00702049	Best of George Strait	$17.99

00702259	Taylor Swift for Easy Guitar	$15.99
00359800	Taylor Swift – Easy Guitar Anthology	$24.99
00702260	Taylor Swift — Fearless	$14.99
00139727	Taylor Swift — 1989	$17.99
00115960	Taylor Swift — Red	$16.99
00253667	Taylor Swift — Reputation	$17.99
00702290	Taylor Swift — Speak Now	$16.99
00232849	Chris Tomlin Collection – 2nd Edition	$14.99
00702226	Chris Tomlin — See the Morning	$12.95
00148643	Train	$14.99
00702427	U2 — 18 Singles	$19.99
00702108	Best of Stevie Ray Vaughan	$17.99
00279005	The Who	$14.99
00702123	Best of Hank Williams	$15.99
00194548	Best of John Williams	$14.99
00702228	Neil Young — Greatest Hits	$17.99
00119133	Neil Young — Harvest	$14.99

Prices, contents and availability subject to change without notice.

HAL•LEONARD®

Visit Hal Leonard online at **halleonard.com**

1221
306

GUITAR PLAY-ALONG

INCLUDES TAB
AUDIO ACCESS INCLUDED

This series will help you play your favorite songs quickly and easily. Just follow the tab and listen to the audio to hear how the guitar should sound, and then play along using the separate backing tracks.

Playback tools are provided for slowing down the tempo without changing pitch and looping challenging parts. The melody and lyrics are included in the book so that you can sing or simply follow along.

105. LATIN
00700939.............................$16.99

106. WEEZER
00700958.............................$14.99

107. CREAM
00701069.............................$16.99

108. THE WHO
00701053.............................$16.99

109. STEVE MILLER
00701054.............................$19.99

110. SLIDE GUITAR HITS
00701055.............................$16.99

111. JOHN MELLENCAMP
00701056.............................$14.99

112. QUEEN
00701052.............................$16.99

113. JIM CROCE
00701058.............................$17.99

114. BON JOVI
00701060.............................$16.99

115. JOHNNY CASH
00701070.............................$16.99

116. THE VENTURES
00701124.............................$17.99

117. BRAD PAISLEY
00701224.............................$16.99

118. ERIC JOHNSON
00701353.............................$16.99

119. AC/DC CLASSICS
00701356.............................$17.99

120. PROGRESSIVE ROCK
00701457.............................$14.99

121. U2
00701508.............................$16.99

122. CROSBY, STILLS & NASH
00701610.............................$16.99

123. LENNON & McCARTNEY ACOUSTIC
00701614.............................$16.99

124. SMOOTH JAZZ
00200664.............................$16.99

125. JEFF BECK
00701687.............................$17.99

126. BOB MARLEY
00701701.............................$17.99

127. 1970S ROCK
00701739.............................$16.99

128. 1960S ROCK
00701740.............................$14.99

129. MEGADETH
00701741.............................$17.99

130. IRON MAIDEN
00701742.............................$17.99

131. 1990S ROCK
00701743.............................$14.99

132. COUNTRY ROCK
00701757.............................$15.99

133. TAYLOR SWIFT
00701894.............................$16.99

134. AVENGED SEVENFOLD
00701906.............................$16.99

135. MINOR BLUES
00151350.............................$17.99

136. GUITAR THEMES
00701922.............................$14.99

137. IRISH TUNES
00701966.............................$15.99

138. BLUEGRASS CLASSICS
00701967.............................$17.99

139. GARY MOORE
00702370.............................$16.99

140. MORE STEVIE RAY VAUGHAN
00702396.............................$17.99

141. ACOUSTIC HITS
00702401.............................$16.99

142. GEORGE HARRISON
00237697.............................$17.99

143. SLASH
00702425.............................$19.99

144. DJANGO REINHARDT
00702531.............................$16.99

145. DEF LEPPARD
00702532.............................$19.99

146. ROBERT JOHNSON
00702533.............................$16.99

147. SIMON & GARFUNKEL
14041591.............................$16.99

148. BOB DYLAN
14041592.............................$16.99

149. AC/DC HITS
14041593.............................$17.99

150. ZAKK WYLDE
02501717.............................$19.99

151. J.S. BACH
02501730.............................$16.99

152. JOE BONAMASSA
02501751.............................$19.99

153. RED HOT CHILI PEPPERS
00702990.............................$19.99

155. ERIC CLAPTON – FROM THE ALBUM UNPLUGGED
00703085.............................$16.99

156. SLAYER
00703770.............................$19.99

157. FLEETWOOD MAC
00101382.............................$17.99

159. WES MONTGOMERY
00102593.............................$19.99

160. T-BONE WALKER
00102641.............................$17.99

161. THE EAGLES – ACOUSTIC
00102659.............................$17.99

162. THE EAGLES HITS
00102667.............................$17.99

163. PANTERA
00103036.............................$17.99

164. VAN HALEN 1986-1995
00110270.............................$17.99

165. GREEN DAY
00210343.............................$17.99

166. MODERN BLUES
00700764.............................$16.99

167. DREAM THEATER
00111938.............................$24.99

168. KISS
00113421.............................$17.99

169. TAYLOR SWIFT
00115982.............................$16.99

170. THREE DAYS GRACE
00117337.............................$16.99

171. JAMES BROWN
00117420.............................$16.99

172. THE DOOBIE BROTHERS
00116970.............................$16.99

173. TRANS-SIBERIAN ORCHESTRA
00119907.............................$19.99

174. SCORPIONS
00122119.............................$16.99

175. MICHAEL SCHENKER
00122127.............................$17.99

176. BLUES BREAKERS WITH JOHN MAYALL & ERIC CLAPTON
00122132.............................$19.99

177. ALBERT KING
00123271.............................$16.99

178. JASON MRAZ
00124165.............................$17.99

179. RAMONES
00127073.............................$16.99

180. BRUNO MARS
00129706.............................$16.99

181. JACK JOHNSON
00129854.............................$16.99

182. SOUNDGARDEN
00138161.............................$17.99

183. BUDDY GUY
00138240.............................$17.99

184. KENNY WAYNE SHEPHERD
00138258.............................$17.99

185. JOE SATRIANI
00139457.............................$17.99

186. GRATEFUL DEAD
00139459.............................$17.99

187. JOHN DENVER
00140839.............................$17.99

188. MÖTLEY CRUE
00141145.............................$17.99

189. JOHN MAYER
00144350.............................$17.99

190. DEEP PURPLE
00146152.............................$17.99

191. PINK FLOYD CLASSICS
00146164.............................$17.99

192. JUDAS PRIEST
00151352.............................$17.99

193. STEVE VAI
00156028.............................$19.99

194. PEARL JAM
00157925.............................$17.99

195. METALLICA: 1983-1988
00234291.............................$19.99

196. METALLICA: 1991-2016
00234292.............................$19.99

HAL•LEONARD®

For complete songlists, visit
Hal Leonard online at
www.halleonard.com

Prices, contents, and availability subject to
change without notice.

1120
9/12; 397

easy GUITAR play along

Audio Access Included

INCLUDES TAB

The *Easy Guitar Play Along®* series features streamlined transcriptions of your favorite songs. Just follow the tab, listen to the audio to hear how the guitar should sound, and then play along using the backing tracks. Playback tools are provided for slowing down the tempo without changing pitch and looping challenging parts. The melody and lyrics are included in the book so that you can sing or simply follow along.

1. ROCK CLASSICS
Jailbreak • Living After Midnight • Mississippi Queen • Rocks Off • Runnin' Down a Dream • Smoke on the Water • Strutter • Up Around the Bend.
00702560 Book/CD Pack....... $14.99

2. ACOUSTIC TOP HITS
About a Girl • I'm Yours • The Lazy Song • The Scientist • 21 Guns • Upside Down • What I Got • Wonderwall.
00702569 Book/CD Pack....... $14.99

3. ROCK HITS
All the Small Things • Best of You • Brain Stew (The Godzilla Remix) • Californication • Island in the Sun • Plush • Smells Like Teen Spirit • Use Somebody.
00702570 Book/CD Pack....... $14.99

4. ROCK 'N' ROLL
Blue Suede Shoes • I Get Around • I'm a Believer • Jailhouse Rock • Oh, Pretty Woman • Peggy Sue • Runaway • Wake Up Little Susie.
00702572 Book/CD Pack $14.99

6. CHRISTMAS SONGS
Have Yourself a Merry Little Christmas • A Holly Jolly Christmas • The Little Drummer Boy • Run Rudolph Run • Santa Claus Is Comin' to Town • Silver and Gold • Sleigh Ride • Winter Wonderland.
00101879 Book/CD Pack......... $14.99

7. BLUES SONGS FOR BEGINNERS
Come On (Part 1) • Double Trouble • Gangster of Love • I'm Ready • Let Me Love You Baby • Mary Had a Little Lamb • San-Ho-Zay • T-Bone Shuffle.
00103235 Book/
     Online Audio..........$17.99

9. ROCK SONGS FOR BEGINNERS
Are You Gonna Be My Girl • Buddy Holly • Everybody Hurts • In Bloom • Otherside • The Rock Show • Santa Monica • When I Come Around.
00103255 Book/CD Pack.....$14.99

10. GREEN DAY
Basket Case • Boulevard of Broken Dreams • Good Riddance (Time of Your Life) • Holiday • Longview • 21 Guns • Wake Me up When September Ends • When I Come Around.
00122322 Book/CD Pack $14.99

11. NIRVANA
All Apologies • Come As You Are • Heart Shaped Box • Lake of Fire • Lithium • The Man Who Sold the World • Rape Me • Smells Like Teen Spirit.
00122325 Book/
     Online Audio $17.99

13. AC/DC
Back in Black • Dirty Deeds Done Dirt Cheap • For Those About to Rock (We Salute You) • Hells Bells • Highway to Hell • Rock and Roll Ain't Noise Pollution • T.N.T. • You Shook Me All Night Long.
14042895 Book/
     Online Audio........ $17.99

14. JIMI HENDRIX – SMASH HITS
All Along the Watchtower • Can You See Me • Crosstown Traffic • Fire • Foxey Lady • Hey Joe • Manic Depression • Purple Haze • Red House • Remember • Stone Free • The Wind Cries Mary.
00130591 Book/
     Online Audio........$24.99

HAL•LEONARD®
www.halleonard.com

Prices, contents, and availability subject to change without notice.